SELECTED LISTENING

With Dizzy Gillespie:

Dee Gee Days (1951–52), Savoy SV4426 CD.

With Thelonious Monk:

Thelonious Monk with John Coltrane (1957), Original Jazz Classics OJC 039 CD.

With Miles Davis:

Kind of Blue (1959), Columbia CK 40579 CD.

John Coltrane Quartet:

Giant Steps (1959), Atlantic A2 1311 CD.

My Favorite Things (1961), Atlantic 1361 CD.

Africa/Brass (1961), Impulse! MCAD 42001 CD.

Impressions (1961–63), Impulse! MCAD 5887 CD.

A Love Supreme (1964), Impulse! GRD 155 CD.

FURTHER READING

Barron, Rachel Stiffler. *John Coltrane: Jazz Revolutionary.* Greensboro, NC: Morgan Reynolds Publishing, 2002.

The John Coltrane Foundation–Jowcol Music. www.johncoltrane.com (27 January 2007).

Raschka, Chris. *John Coltrane's Giant Steps.* New York: Richard Jackson Books/Atheneum, 2002.

Selfridge, John. *John Coltrane: A Sound Supreme.* New York: Franklin Watts, 1999.

AUTHOR'S NOTE

Legendary jazz saxophonist JOHN COLTRANE (1926–67) was born in Hamlet, North Carolina, and raised in High Point, North Carolina, where his grandfather was a minister in the African Methodist Episcopal Zion Church. John, his parents, aunt, uncle, and cousin Mary all lived with his grandparents. His mother, who wanted to be an opera singer, played piano for the church choir. His father, a tailor, enjoyed playing violin and ukulele and singing country music. When the scout leader, the church's assistant pastor, formed a community band, John, then twelve, began playing clarinet. Around the same time, his grandmother, grandfather, aunt, and father died. Their deaths hit the family hard. John's grades suffered, and his mother had money troubles. She rented rooms to boarders. She eventually went to Philadelphia—along with her sister and niece—to find work, leaving John behind with the boarders.

John poured himself into his music. He played in the school band and spent all his spare time playing. After hearing jazz on the radio, he began playing the alto saxophone. His class voted him Most Musical and Best Dressed. Upon high school graduation, John moved to Philadelphia to be closer to his mother. There, he continued his musical training. Drafted into the military during World War II, he played in the U.S. Navy Band. After the war, stints with the Eddie "Cleanhead" Vinson Band and with Jimmy Heath broadened Coltrane's musical horizons and sparked his passion for experimentation.

His musical evolution continued with the bands of pianist/composer Thelonious Monk and trumpeter Dizzy Gillespie, both bebop pioneers, and trumpeter Miles Davis, a jazz innovator. With the Miles Davis Quintet in the late 1950s, Coltrane developed a unique three-on-one chord approach by playing multiple notes at the same time, a technique since called "sheets of sound." During that period, he also played with the bands of Cannonball Adderley and others. Sadly, he abused drugs and alcohol, addictions from which he later broke free.

With a growing reputation as a composer and improvising tenor saxophonist, he bought a soprano saxophone in 1960 and formed the John Coltrane Quartet. That group revolutionized jazz with such recordings as *Giant Steps*, *My Favorite Things*, *Africa/Brass*, *Impressions*, and *A Love Supreme*. Toward the end of his career, Coltrane developed radical musical styles, explored spiritual themes, incorporated Indian instruments and African percussion, and supported young musicians. In 1967, he died at the age of forty of liver disease.

Today, Coltrane's music can still be heard in movies and on television and radio. In 1995, the United States Postal Service issued a stamp in his honor.

he

was

all

ears.

Before John was a jazz giant,

blew into the mouthpiece,
pressed his fingers on the keys,
and breathed every sound
he'd ever known into a bold new song.

Before John was a jazz giant,

he picked up that horn,

Before John was a jazz giant,
he heard big bands on the radio
and a saxophone's soulful solo,
blue notes crooning his name.

Before John was a jazz giant,
he heard birds warbling at sunrise,
the sobs of kinfolk at family funerals,
and cheers as he marched in parades.

Before John was a jazz giant,
he heard Grandpa's Sunday sermons,
Mama playing hymns for the senior choir,
and the scoutmaster's call to join a band.

Before John was a jazz giant,
he heard steam engines whistling past,
Cousin Mary giggling at jitterbuggers,
and Bojangles tap-dancing in the picture show.

he heard hambones knocking in Grandma's pots,
Daddy strumming the ukulele,
and Mama cranking the phonograph.

Before John was a jazz giant,

To Ron and Mommy with love

To the memory of Great-aunt Terah,
Coltrane's third-grade teacher,
and Aunt Terah, a jazz-loving librarian
—C. B. W.

To the memory of my father,
Edward Jewel Qualls,
with whom I shared a love of music,
and as always to Selina and Isaiah
—S. Q.

SQUARE

FISH

An imprint of Macmillan Publishing Group, LLC
120 Broadway, New York, NY 10271
mackids.com
Text copyright © 2008 by Carole Boston Weatherford.
Illustrations copyright © 2008 by Sean Qualls
All rights reserved.
Square Fish and the Square Fish logo are trademarks of Macmillan and are used by
Henry Holt and Company under license from Macmillan.
Our books may be purchased in bulk for promotional, educational, or business use.
Please contact your local bookseller or the Macmillan Corporate and
Premium Sales Department at (800) 221-7945 ext. 5442 or by email
at MacmillanSpecialMarkets@macmillan.com.

The Library of Congress has cataloged the hardcover edition as follows:
Weatherford, Carole Boston.
Before John was a jazz giant : a song of John Coltrane / by Carole Boston Weatherford;
illustrated by Sean Qualls.—1st ed.
p. cm.
ISBN 978-1-250-82270-3 (paperback)
1. Coltrane, John, 1926–1967—Juvenile literature. 2. Jazz musicians—United States—
Biography—Juvenile literature. 3. Saxophonists—United States—Biography—Juvenile literature.
I. Qualls, Sean. II. Title.
ML3930.C535W43 2008 788.7´165092—dc22 [B] 2007007196
Originally published in the United States by Henry Holt and Company
First Square Fish edition, 2022
Book designed by Laurent Linn
Square Fish logo designed by Filomena Tuosto
Printed in China.
1 3 5 7 9 10 8 6 4 2
AR: 3.8 / LEXILE: AD1090L

Before John Was a Jazz Giant

A Song of John Coltrane

Carole Boston Weatherford

illustrated by Sean Qualls

SQUARE
FISH

HENRY HOLT AND COMPANY • NEW YORK